The Ice Break

An opera in three acts
by

MICHAEL TIPPETT

T0081264

Edition 11253a

SCHOTT & CO. LTD., LONDON
48 Great Marlborough Street, London W1V 2BN
B. Schott's Söhne, Mainz
Schott Music Corporation, New York

DRAMATIS PERSONAE

LEV	50 year old teacher; released after 20 years prison and exile	*Bass*
NÁDIA	His wife; who emigrated with their baby son	*Lyric Soprano*
YURI	Their son; a student and second generation immigrant	*Baritone*
GAYLE	Yuri's present and native-born white girl friend	*Dramatic Soprano*
HANNAH	Gayle's black friend; a hospital nurse	*Rich Mezzo*
OLYMPION	Hannah's boy friend; a black champion	*Tenor*
LUKE	A young intern at Hannah's hospital	*Tenor*
LIEUTENANT	A lieutenant of Police	*Baritone*
ASTRON	A psychedelic messenger	*Lyric Mezzo & High Tenor (or Counter Tenor)*
CHORUS	of various groups	

NOTE

CHORUS

The chorus is always anonymous, whatever group it represents. It must be masked in some form, not only to enforce anonymity, but so that the stage representation is unrelated to the singers' real body, in the sense that, for example, the traditional black-and-white ministrels might be played by Chinese. The masking is also necessary to show that stereotypes altogether are in question, rather than any presently exacerbated example e.g. 'black and white'. In a chorus scene the whole stage is occupied and any extant non-chorus scene totally submerged, even though when the chorus goes, the non-chorus scene appears once more still in progress. From this it follows that however much the dramatic action seems to move at times towards verisimilitude, this stage 'reality' is constantly splintered by a complimentary 'surrealism'. To obtain the imperatively necessary histrionic vitality in the chorus scenes, non-singing performers may have to be used. Indeed it might be possible, if it were appropriate, to separate the true oral source of vocal sound from the imagined, or histrionic source, altogether.

MUSIC

In the music there are two archetypal sounds; one related to the frightening but exhilarating sound of the ice breaking on the great northern rivers in the spring; the other related to the exciting or terrifying sound of the slogan-shouting crowds, which can lift you on their shoulders in triumph or stamp you to death.

THE LANGUAGE

When Lev and Nadia converse together in English and not in their mother-tongue, that is literary convention. With other characters the slang English used at times is closer to North American usage than, say, British or Australian.

Broad or open vowels are indicated by an ′ over the letter, thus:

á   as in cast
é   as in crate
í   as in cheese
ó   as in coat
ú   as in coot

'Frères humains, qui après nous vivez,
n'ayer les coeurs contre nous endurcis.'

'Brother humans, who will live after us,
do not harden your hearts against us.'

Commissioned by the Royal Opera House,
Covent Garden.

to Colin Davis

ACT 1

SCENE 1

(The hum of a vast airport lounge-hall)

NADIA Years back,
When I first brought you to this land,
We came by ship.
O those terrifying waves!
Now he comes to us by plane.
Your father flies to us like a homing-bird.
He won't fear those terrifying waves!

YURI *(Shouting above some incoherent
announcement over the loudspeakers)*

He won't see them; he'll be too high.

NADIA Aren't you excited, Yuri?
To see your father.
Twenty years of camp and exile.

YURI No. I can't remember.

NADIA I remember,
As it were yesterday.
I see him always.
I see him now,
Flying to us like a bird.

YURI *(Half-shouting)*

Keep your feet on this earth, momma!

NADIA I see him. I hear him.
He's speaking to me now.
Lev. Lev. what is it?

YURI *(Over another burst of the loudspeakers)*

O Jesus Christ!

LEV	*(off-stage through the loudspeakers where the scrambled announcement gives way to his voice)*
	I came from exile in the spring, As the ice was breaking on the rivers. I've heard that sound so many years upon years of despair; But now with hope. O my Nadia: Do you remember how we sauntered by the flowing river?
NADIA	I remember, I remember.
LEV	How we hugged and kissed in the spring sunshine?
NADIA	I remember, I remember.
	(The airport hum takes over from Lev's voice on the speakers and swamps Nadia's)

SCENE 2

GAYLE	Look, Hannah, there's young Yuri. Hi, Yuri, why here? How come?
YURI	*(Bitterly)*
	My mother's over there: In one of her trances. We've come to meet my father.
GAYLE	I never knew you had a father.
HANNAH	O yes, he has. Nadia has often told me. Years of prison for some no-crime.
YURI	Do me a favour: Keep your nose clean of my affairs. And that was years ago when I was three.
	(Half-shouted)
	Cowards, they let themselves be stamped on.

(Natural voice)

We're different now.

GAYLE
You needn't shout our Hannah down,
She's on the world's top.
Hail to Olympion, the hero.
"Ain't that so", Hannah?

HANNAH
My man flies home in triumph.

GAYLE
Look out! The fans!

SCENE 3

(The fans, mostly black, some white, fill the stage, submerging everything, shouting and dancing, with rattles and toy-trumpets, the latter possibly pre-taped over the loudspeakers)

FANS
Olá, Oló, Olympion!

(Some voices shouted)

Yeh! Yeh!
Hi-ya, Hannah, hi-ya.
Olá, Oló, Olympion!
Yeh! Yeh!
Come on, Gayle.
Let's go!

(When they go they sweep Hannah away with them)

SCENE 4

YURI
Gayle, stop!
Why d'you fool around with Hannah and the blacks?

GAYLE
What's bugging you man?
Cool and jivey once;
Now, touchy and tight.
You're a drag, Hannah's with it — and the others.

(The loudspeakers announce an arrival. Gayle hurries after Hannah and the fans)

YURI *(As though shouting after her)*
And Olympion, that black bastard.

SCENE 5

(The airport hum takes over. Yuri stands sullen and pensive till Nadia jogs him)

NADIA Yuri, Yuri, I need you.

YURI *(Inattentive, as though with his ears cocked for sounds from fans off-stage)*
What is it?

NADIA Is the plane late?

YURI Probably.
Have they announced it?

NADIA Where were you? Who were you with?

YURI Gayle and Hannah.

NADIA Is the plane late?

YURI Probably.
Have they announced it?
(Off-stage cheering)

NADIA What's all that cheering?
Is it for Lev?

YURI No. Olympion.

NADIA Is the plane late?

YURI *(Half-shouting, directly at his mother, in exasperation)*
I don't know.

SCENE 6

(The stage is once more submerged by the fans, returning with Olympion, Gayle and Hannah)

FANS   Olá, Oló
                        (shouted)
                        Yeh! Yeh!
                        *(A cheer-leader and some of the fans
                        prepare to put on one of those half-
                        embarrassing, half-comic, cheer-leader acts)*

CHEER-
LEADER &
FANS   *(Throwing their bodies from side to side)*
                        Olí ... Olá ... Oló
                        Olú, Olympion.
                        Our ché, chá, chá, chú, chí,
                        Our champion.

OLYMPION   *(Acknowledging the act with flamboyant
                        good-humour)*
                        I'm beautiful: I'm black:
                        I am unbeatable.

FANS   Champion!

OLYMPION   I'm beautiful: I'm black:
                        I am unbeatable.
                        "Ain't that so", Hannah?

HANNAH   "Sure is so," Olympion.

OLYMPION   "Ain't that so," Gayle?

GAYLE   "Sure is so," Olympion.

FANS   Olá, Oló
                        (shouted)
                        Yeh! Yeh!
                        *(As the stage clears of fans and their hero,
                        the hum of the airport lounge takes over)*

SCENE 7

(Nadia finds herself alone, for Yuri has gone. She looks round in great distress. A soberly dressed man, clearly a traveller, is watching her. When their eyes at last meet, there is a slow recognition)

LEV

Nadia, Nadia,
I am your husband.

NADIA

Lev, my little Lev,
You flew to me like a bird.

(They embrace. Behind the music the airport lounge dissolves into . . . .

SCENE 8

. . . . Nadia's tiny apartment, where she and Lev can feel as intimate as they need)

NADIA

And the camps? the prison? the exile?
Ah, I should have stayed there with you:
Tho' I saw this country in a vision.

LEV

No, no — You saw right.
We alone survived the camps
who had no ties, no family.
But you and . . .

(scanning her face)

You were safe.
Was it hard?

NADIA

At first.
No dream, Lev,
A rough country.
But we . . .

(Checking herself in apprehension, then hurrying on)

Not cruel like it was there for you.
Alive! a miracle!

LEV

Poetry upheld me.

(Quoting)

'The earth was worth ten heavens to us.'

NADIA

I dreamed of heaven.
But when he,
when he grew up, the earth was kinder.

LEV

So Yuri is grown-up.
What kind of man?

NADIA

(Crying out)

Do not ask me, Lev.
What does father or mother
mean to him?

SCENE 9

*(The stage is once more submerged by the
fans, with Hannah, Olympion, Gayle and
Yuri. There is food, probably, certainly
drink. The cheer-leader does his act with
his group)*

FANS

(shouted)

Yeh, Yeh, Yeh, Yeh.

(throwing their bodies from side to side)

Olí ... Olá ... Oló
Olú ... Olympion
Our ché chá chá chú chí,
Our champion.

OLYMPION

*(acknowledging the act with flamboyant
good humour)*

I'm beautiful: I'm black.
I am unbeatable.
"Ain't that so," Hannah?

HANNAH

"Sure is so," Olympion.

OLYMPION

"Ain't that so," Gayle?

GAYLE

"Sure is so," Olympion.

OLYMPION

"Ain't that so," Yuri?

FANS	Answer! Answer! Yeh, Yeh, Yeh, Yeh! Answer! Answer! Yeh Yeh Yeh Yeh Yeh Yeh!
OLYMPION	Screw him, he's a loser! What can that cat do to me, ...
FANS	Nothing, But nothing.
OLYMPION	. . . . the greatest?
FANS	Mighty Olympion, The black man's champion.
OLYMPION	My folks have lived this land More years than any Paddy-Ivan.
FANS	A-ha!
OLYMPION	My folks have lived this land Most years 'slong as Waspy-Whitey.*
FANS	O-ho!
OLYMPION	So now we want our birth-right.
FANS	Yeh, Yeh, Yeh, Yeh.
OLYMPION	Who will claim it?
FANS	Mighty Olympion, the black man's champion.
OLYMPION	I am the greatest.

---

*W.A.S.P. : White Anglo-Saxon Protestant

FANS   Yeh, Yeh, Yeh, Yeh.

OLYMPION   The Lord's a black man.

FANS   Yeh, Yeh, Yeh, Yeh, Yeh, Yeh.

OLYMPION   And whitey gotta pay.

FANS   Pay!

OLYMPION   "Ain't that so," Hannah?

HANNAH   "Maybe is so," Olympion.

OLYMPION   "Ain't that so," Gayle?

GAYLE   "Sure is so," Olympion.

YURI   *(Unable to contain himself in bitter mockery)*

                "Sure is so," Olympion!

                (Bit by bit the White fans have stopped the slogan-singing and have drawn together in a small group with Yuri)

WHITES   Get her away, Yuri,
                Get her away.

GAYLE   *(singing high over everyone present)*

                Olympion,
                Your people have lived this land
                as long as mine,
                Olympion
                But not in freedom: not as equals:
                Not with love.
                That's past, Olympion:
                I make amends.
                We are the new New World.
                "Make love not war."
                And as a pledge, Olympion,
                Come kiss me now, black beauty,
                Kiss.

OLYMPION	*(half-recoiling, half-desiring)* Wow! this chick wants balling?
BLACKS	Ball her, Olympion, ball her.
HANNAH	Gayle's runnin' wild, A devil's in her . . . .
BLACKS	Ball her, Olympion, ball her. Massa balls his slave. Ho! Ho! Ho! Ho!
HANNAH	. . . . Take command, Olympion, Take command; Before the devil's in us too And we all go under.
WHITES	Get her away, Go for him! Get her away, Go for him! Drag her away! Go for the nigger! Drag her away! Go for the nigger!
GAYLE	I make amends, Superstar Olympion, I make amends. *(Gayle goes down on her knees before Olympion and her hair would seem to cover his feet)*
YURI	*(Manic with rage)* You mother-fucking bastard. *(Yuri goes for Olympion, who, without moving, lands him one on the jaw, so that Yuri falls flat. Olympion looks down for a moment at Gayle, then kicks her off with one clean movement)*
OLYMPION	Trash!
BLACKS	Out! out! Whitey out, Whitey out! Out, out! Whitey out, whitey out! Out out out out out out out out Ou-t!

SCENE 10   *(Nadia's apartment)*

NADIA   He is so strange these days:
                   Now dead, now wild.

LEV   Where is he now?

NADIA   I wouldn't know.
                   I used to.
                   But I love him, Lev,
                   I love him.
                   And you will love him.

LEV   For sure.

NADIA   And you will help him.

LEV   For sure, Nadia, for sure.

CHORUS   *(Off-stage)*

                   Out out out out out out out!
                   Ou-t!

                   *(Yuri bursts in dragging Gayle with him. He
                   stares at his father almost with hatred)*

YURI   What have you come here for?

                   CURTAIN

ACT 2

SCENE 1

*(The city at night. As soon as the stage be-
comes visible, showing the apartment, Lev,
Nadia, Yuri and Gayle at once start
singing together, each in their private
world)*

LEV   *(Quoting)*

' . . . Who am I to bear the burdens
of this world:
to be the boss,
the navel of the earth,
let alone the salt . . .'

NADIA   Crazy and cruel now the earth is.
Like him
I have hoped. I have endured
In the dungeons of this town.
Because I see the river
Shining with light as it cleaves the forest.

GAYLE   For me no no bible-belted-safe plantation.
Footloose, I
(With my lover along)
Fool around
For kicks!

YURI   To hell with where one's born!
Haven't I grown to be a man here?
So, listen, while I shout in your
stuffed ears:
Stop crowding me!

LEV   *(breaking out of the ensemble)*
Let me speak.
Violence is blind.
Brutality takes over.
I have experience.

YURI

You've no experience.
Twenty years locked up because you
wouldn't fight.
Here it's different.
We're not pushed around.
Every guy has a gun.

MEN'S VOICES

(Off-stage echoing through the speakers)
Every guy has a gun,
has a gun, has a gun.

LEV

(Quoting)

'. . . Who am I to bear the burdens
of this world:
to be the boss,
the navel of the earth,
let alone the salt . . . '

NADIA

Crazy and cruel now the earth is.
Like him
I have hoped, I have endured
In the dungeons of this town.
Because I see the river,
Shining with light as it cleaves the forest.

GAYLE

For me no bible-belted-safe plantation.
Footloose, I
(With my lover along)
Fool around
For kicks!

YURI

To hell with where one's born!
Haven't I grown to be a man here?
So, listen, while I shout in your
stuffed ears:
Stop crowding me!

GAYLE

(breaking out of the ensemble)

No dream now of liberal charity.
Now is for real.
'Burn, baby, burn!'

WOMEN'S VOICES	*(Off-stage echoing through the speakers)* Burn, baby, burn, baby, burn, baby, burn.
GAYLE	What does that mean? That I be killed? We'll fight first.
LEV	The others can say all that: for ever. So the toughest bully wins. You, how brutal can *you* be?
YURI	Listen to the preaching teacher. You can't teach us.
GAYLE & YURI	We're through Now is for real.
NADIA	Crazy and cruel now the earth is. *(The assembly call at first rivets their attentions; then Gayle and Yuri, as in a ritual, put on the hoods)*
NADIA	*(Crying out with visionary intensity)* I see, I see The Dance of Death Whirling over the city. Who dies? Who dies? *(Nadia goes. The two hooded figures begin perhaps to recede, but always visible and facing the audience. Lev seems to be left behind, alone)*
LEV	*(Quoting)* 'A frozen foot-cloth is the scarf that binds my face.'

SCENE 2

(As the masked figures of Gayle and Yuri move backwards, a similarly masked white chorus moves forward. They all meet and leave the stage.)

CHORUS OF
WHITES

We meet with cordial greetings
in this our sacred cave
to pledge anew our compact,
with hearts sincere and brave.
A band of pure Caucasians,
the noblest of the klan,
we stand in rank together,
white woman with white —

SCENE 3

(Olympion and Hannah are alone, as though in some other part of the night city)

OLYMPION

I must go with them.
If they "walk tall", I walk taller.
I am their god, their hero.
I'm their man.

HANNAH

And I'm a woman.
But no, no.
Stranger and deeper why I stay.

HANNAH &
OLYMPION

What is so strange and deep as love,
Lover leaning to lover in the spring.

OLYMPION

Desert our brothers in trouble.
Run out on them?
Afraid to tangle with Whitey
now the heat is on?

HANNAH

Whitey is human too.
But no, no:
Too glib, too pat.
Stranger and deeper into myself.

HANNAH &
OLYMPION

What is so strange and deep as love,
Lover leaning to lover in the spring.

OLYMPION	Come with me, my babe, my honey, My Hannah, come with me.
CHORUS OF BLACKS	*(As though shouting and singing in the distance and coming nearer)* Out, Out! Out, out, out, out, out, out. Whitey out, Whitey out.
HANNAH	But is it you, Olympion, Is it you, within this mob?

SCENE 4

*(As Hannah cries her last question the
black masked chorus appears to surge onto
the stage. They surround Olympion and
ceremoniously mask him into one of the
mob)*

CHORUS OF BLACKS	Hi, there, black man! Olympion! Hi, there, black man! Olympion! Hi, there, black man! Our fist, our boot, our hammer. Our fist, our boot, our hammer. He'll flick that Whitey out; He'll flick that Whitey out.

*(The masked chorus prepares to surge, or
march, off taking Olympion, now in-
distinguishable, with them. The effect is of
a crowd disappearing rapidly into the
distance)*

CHORUS OF BLACKS	Out, out, Whitey out, Whitey out. Out, out, Whitey out, Whitey out, Out, out, out, out, out, out. Burn, baby, burn! Burn, baby, −

SCENE 5

HANNAH	Stranger and darker Deeper into myself.

Blue night of my soul
Blue-black within this city's night
I scrabble for unformed letters
That might make a word
To speak sense
To the blue night of my soul
Blue-black within this city's night.
But no.
No time, is yet, for sense
Alone,
Deep in the body:
Dark in the soul:
An incommunicable voice murmuring:
Not that, only not that.

CHORUS OF   *(Off-stage)*
WHITES   . . . the noblest of the klan, . . .

CHORUS OF   *(Off-stage)*
BLACKS   . . . baby, burn! . . .

SCENE 6   *(The hooded or masked mobs of Blacks
                   and Whites appear on the stage from
                   opposite sides to enact the final, sur-
                   realist process of tribalisation)*

CHORUS OF
BLACKS   . . . Burn, baby, burn!

CHORUS OF
WHITES   . . . We stand in rank together,
                       white woman with white . . . .

                   (the tribal dancing begins)

CHORUS OF   Wá-wá-wá-wá-wá-wá-white
WHITES   wá-wá-wá-wá-wá-wá-woman
                   with wá-wá-wá-wá-wá-wá-white

CHORUS OF   B, b, b, b, b, burn
BLACKS   b, b, b, b, b, baby
                   b, b, b, b, b, b, b, b, b,
                   burn!

SCENE 7

> *(Lev and Nadia in the apartment. They have temporarily lost all certainty, whether of vision or philosophy. They mutter together in a kind of cat's-cradle of unspoken tensions)*

NADIA   *(half-spoken, half-sung)*

Who dies, who dies?

Alas, alas
I cannot see

For the inner eye is

gotten shut
Tight, blind,
By the weird power
that lifts them open.
And if I saw who dies
How could I hurl a
warning
Cross the blank gulf from

age to youth.
Who would heed?

Lev, Lev, it falls to you.

LEV "No dream of liberal
charity", she said.
"Now is for real"
Is her passion then
more real than my
patience?
Must I despise the
liberal
charity
I live by?
I have no gun.

I cannot shoot.
But they, with fierce
vitality,
They shoot each
other.

Or if they could
together
Shoot away this
rotten world . . .?
I go with my bare
hands.

> *(Lev rushes out into the night)*

SCENE 8

> *(The Black mob have someone from the White mob on the ground, writhing and crawling, and are kicking him to death. Each entry of the boot proceeds with a*

heavy thud and scream (amplified if need be by other voices) from the body on the ground. Some revolver shots from one side. The Blacks scatter except one, to the other side. This single figure stays beside the prostrate body on the stage to deliver the final blow. Another shot brings him to the ground.

Some Whites begin to creep forward from their side. One shot from the Black side of the stage. The Whites scurry to shelter except one, more imprudent than the rest, who reaches the first prostrate body and perhaps even tries to lift or drag it. Prolonged volley of shots from the Black side of the stage; perhaps even from a sub-machine gun. The White figure falls.

Police-car and ambulance sirens coming nearer and louder from the distance, till the headlamps are visible and we know that the cars have stopped and the personnel have got out)

SCENE 9

(The Lieutenant of Police strides down stage towards the audience)

LIEUTENANT

(Through loud-hailer)
Police — or fuzz?
Cops — or pigs?
You take your choice
You on your ass out there.

(Matter-of-fact, natural voice)

Well, Doc Luke,
Who lives? who lives?

LUKE

(beside the black body)
(spoken)
Dead

(The face is unmasked as Hannah comes closer)

Olympion!

(To Hannah)

O you poor bastards,
"Gone with the wind."

(shouting)

For what?

HANNAH   What has more power of pain than love?

LIEUTENANT   To the mortuary!

(through loud-hailer to the world at large)

Trash!

(Olympion's body is removed)

LUKE   *(beside the second white body that fell)*
(spoken)

Dead

(The face is unmasked)

Gayle!
The kid who died for kicks.
Gayle, bonny Gayle,
gone out with the wind.

LIEUTENANT   To the mortuary!

(through the loud-hailer to the world at large)
Trash!

(Gayle's body is removed. Luke is beside the third body which is finally unmasked)

LEV   *(rushing forward)*
Yuri!

LIEUTENANT   Back.
Who are you?

LEV   He is my son.

LIEUTENANT   *(through the loud-hailer to the world at large)*
What a father!

(natural voice to Lev)
Why in a'mighty hell
not have kept him out of this?

LEV   Please, please, is he alive?

LUKE   *(Spat out)*
               If we make the hospital in time,
               He may live . . .
               (bitterly)
               like us all.

LIEUTENANT   Ambulance.

LEV   I will come with you.
               (Yuri is lifted into the ambulance)

LUKE   No: tomorrow.
               Turn to Nurse Hannah.

               *(The cars with their burdens go off with
               sirens wailing into the distance)*

SCENE 10

*(The stage is empty except for the figures
of Lev and Hannah seeking comfort for
their sorrow. Perhaps Lev, as the cello takes
over from the violin for a time, decides to
accept Luke's advice to turn to Hannah.)*

CURTAIN

ACT 3

SCENE 1	*(Nadia is dozing in the apartment. Lev sits beside her reading)*
LEV'S VOICE (murmured)	*(Over the loud-speakers)* 'Now the boat glided in the hot, noonday sunshine, down-stream; gentle breezes . . .'
NADIA	Lev, Lev, when will they come?
LEV	Soon, Nadia, soon. Lie still.
LEV'S VOICE (murmured)	' . . . right above, on the sharpest edge of such a cliff, where otherwise the towpath might have passed . . '
NADIA	*(murmuring)* I cannot lie still.
LEV'S VOICE (murmured)	' . . . saw a young man ride up, well built, of powerful form . . .'
NADIA	Ah, but I need to know if Yuri lives. *(Lev perhaps lays a hand on Nadia's arm to comfort her – but continues to read)*
LEV'S VOICE (murmured)	' . . . but scarcely did they try to see him more clearly, when the overhanging mass there broke loose, and that unlucky youth, horse over rider, plunged down into the water.'

SCENE 2

	(Luke and Hannah have arrived)
NADIA	How is he, doctor?
LUKE	Yuri is fine, just fine. But what of you?

NADIA	Will Yuri walk again Upright like a man?
LUKE	We think so. The test will come later.
NADIA	I shall not see that.
HANNAH	Indeed you will. Rest now: relax. *(Luke takes Lev aside)*
NADIA	My dear soul, You'll look for Lev, When I am gone.
HANNAH	I'll try — but . . .
NADIA	Since that crazed night, And Yuri hov'ring between death and life, I fall away into extinction. But now, but now I see, I see Lev the Lion stand in my place. *(Nadia's face retains the look of visionary ecstasy until the trumpets cease)*

SCENE 3

(Hannah and Lev are together. Luke perhaps is seen leaving)

LEV	*(passionately)* Why did I leave that other country? *(Imitating Yuri's sneering tone end of Act 1)* What have I come here for? *(bitterly)* To watch my wife's death and my son's hatred?
HANNAH	*(very distinct)* That other country has troubles too. Tell me.

LEV

Comrades
  In the camp
Against the brutal guards
  (Few felt them human too)
Totally single for survival.

I licked my wounds
  In Exile
Cringed into country quiet,
  Yet longed for the city.

The town seemed dead,
  Upon release,
The life conformist, empty.

(crying out)   HANNAH
Was Yuri right
We flunked the struggle? Struggle is always,

I ran away   Is here,
               Ev'rywhere in this
               vast world of
               ghettos.

I ran away   How to be reborn
               out of the ghetto?

Ah! Ah!   On what deep
               level?

SCENE 4

(Lev and Hannah are interrupted by the, for them, 'metaphorical' sound of sleigh-bells as Nadia begins her swan-song of death. The aria is fantasy, not realism. Lev and Hannah are present, but out of focus except when they comment)

NADIA

Who holds me tight round the waist,
as the sleigh flies over the snow?
My brother? his school-mate?
Crowds of young comrades ski-ing
skimming round the forest trees
with scarves flying.

I have felt-boots and a padded-coat.
But he holds me tight, warm
as the sleigh stops sharp at the door.
The hot stoves glow red in the house.

LEV How is she, Hannah?

HANNAH Failing: very gently.

NADIA They sleep; I wake.
Dark in the little room before dawn.
The night-light for us younger children has
gone out.
I shan't need a night-light soon
for my body changes.
Ahí, ahí,
Whatever's that?
The ice is breaking on the river.
Máma, Nánya, Lev
Oh come, do come.

LEV Is she in pain, Hannah?

HANNAH No: the body shudders.
Death is near.

NADIA I am walking thro' fields of marguerites
in the hot, hot, summer sun.
They reach my shoulders;
my head peers out above.
Ah, I see far off the forest
and the river.
What a tiny boat!
I glide downstream.
The wide water is full of folk,
Calling, calling . . .

CHORUS *(Off-stage through loud-speakers)*
We are all here,
We are all here.

LEV *(Crying out)*
Nadia, Nadia, wait for me in Paradise.

SCENE 5

(Seekers of all kinds tough and tender, past, present and future, are in the Paradise Garden; perhaps smoking pipes of peace or pot)

CHORUS

Ready?
Am I ready?
Are you ready?
Are we all . . .
. . . ready
for the trip?

(If appropriate they puff out clouds of smoke)

What is that drumming, thrumming in the sky?
What is that rumbling, crumbling in the Earth?
A dadda-momma of a storm within the universe.

We could use
Some good News
From Nowhere right now.

Trekking from the farthest star,
Atoms, with the speed of light,
Assemble incarnate
Here.

(As the psychedelic colours reach their greatest intensity, Astron materialises)

ASTRON

My letter to you is in code, not clear.
A tongue-slip that?
No matter.
'Dear friends,
Take care for the Earth.
God will take care for himself.'

CHORUS

Take care,
Ah take care
For the Earth
Our mother.

ASTRON

A blessing I remember
From an earlier dream:
'Spring come to you at the farthest
In the very end of harvest.'

CHORUS

Astron!
O Messenger!
Angel!
Our Saviour Hero!

ASTRON

(highly ironic: rising into falsetto)

Saviour?! Hero?! Me!!

(natural voice)

You must be joking.

(Astron's psychedelic image starts to tremble and disintegrate to nothing)

(invisible, in the distance, as though from the black hole where he appeared;

ASTRON

through the speakers)

'Take care for the Earth.
God will take care for himself.'

(The Paradise Garden with the Chorus vanishes as by explosion)

SCENE 6

(The quiet of Luke's consulting room. From time to time Lev seems to hear faint musical echoes, inaudible to Luke, from Nadia's death scene)

LUKE	*(distinct, serious but cool)*
	Daily I deal with death . . . and life.
	The seriously sick move towards death,
	Are accepted, are refused.
	Or so it seems.
	My skilled hands sometimes decide.
	Or so it seems.
	In the camps,
	You too lived daily life with death,
	Moved at times, I reckon, very close;
	But were rejected.
	You cannot be where Nadia is.
	You are where Yuri is.
	Your face changes.
	Something has happened?
LEV	Yes.
LUKE	Are you then ready?
LEV	I am ready.

SCENE 7

(Some hall within the hive of activity of a large hospital. (Lev and Luke are possibly still visibly where they were in Scene 6.) Hannah wheels in Yuri, prone on a mobile table. He is totally (at least metaphorically) encased in plaster)

YURI	What happens now, Hannah?
HANNAH	At the crunch, Yuri,
	Shouldn't you call me nurse?
YURI	Nurse Hannah, then.
	What happens now?
HANNAH	We cut the plaster open,
	And see the ghastly white flesh inside.
LUKE	*(approaching in his white coat)*
	Is all set, Nurse?
	And the patient ready?

YURI	Will you make me walk?
LUKE	Not yet; in time.

(Hannah wheels Yuri away into the operating room. Luke follows)

(The quartet-ensemble is surrealism, not realism. Luke, Hannah, Yuri are within (their voices may have to be amplified), operating or suffering, as in some huge shadow-play, an alarming but healing ritual. Lev, now in the hall, is left alone in full view)

LEV
Now his awareness concentrates,
Like waiting for interrogation.
His heart-beats quicken,
As the seconds lengthen in the mind to minutes,
And the minutes into hours.
O Yuri, does one ever walk
Again upright after interrogation?

HANNAH
No anaesthetic:
You'll feel no pain.

LUKE
Relax if possible.
The heart races.

YURI
Had I no nerves,
No apprehension,
All might be simple.
In this extremity
I fall like Momma into trance.

LUKE
Cutter: saw.

HANNAH
I have them ready.

LUKE
Then we begin.

LEV	Now they begin the beautiful operation. With saw and cutter to crack the shell To release the naked human chick And test the skill That soldered my Yuri's crushed bones together. Surely a paean of triumph. O moment of joy!
YURI	Ah-í! Ah-í! Doctor, Nurse, Take care for the fragile body So white appearing. Ah-í! Ah-í! Dead-white and naked. My body is free. Joy, joy, joy! Oy, oy, oy, oy!
LUKE	That plaster there; Wrench it free. Nurse, the cutters! A birth like Caesar's, surely! *(with Hannah in triumph)* The patient is free. The patient is free.
HANNAH	There, I have it. Ripe for the trash can. *(with Luke in triumph)* The patient is free. The patient is free.

SCENE 8

(With voices of Scene 7 still echoing around, the Chorus from the Paradise Garden whirls through the hospital like a carnival rout. Somersaults and cart-wheels would be in order. Large untuned handbells to be clanged in time with the rhythmical words that are projected, as the Chorus enters, maybe through loud-hailers; within a general hum of voices which then take up the singing)

CHORUS

'Spring, spring
Spring come to you at the farthest.
In the very end of harvest.'

SCENE 9

(As the chorus whirls away, Hannah brings a now robed Yuri out of the operating room in a wheeled chair. She wheels him almost up to the standing Lev. Yuri stares at his father intently searching his face)

YURI

(with a touch of authority)

Help me up, Nurse, Doctor.

(Luke and Hannah do so)

YURI

Let me go!
Let me stand!

(Yuri stands, then takes some tentative steps)

YURI

Father!

LEV

Son!

(they embrace)

YURI

Chastened, together,
We try once more.

(drawing himself fully upright)

"Ain't that so", Hannah?

(He topples. Luke and Hannah help him back into the chair)